Finding Out About
RAILWAYS

Sarah Harris

Batsford Academic and Educational Ltd *London*

Contents

Introduction	3
Useful Sources	4
The Early Railways	6
The First Steam Locomotives	7
Building the Railways: Engineers and Contractors	8
Building the Railways: The Navvies	10
Opposition to the Railways	12
The Hidden Cost	14
Shareholders	16
Railway Towns	18
Station Architecture	20
Travelling on the Railways: The Not So Rich and The Poor	22
Travelling on the Railways: The Rich	24
A Day Out	26
Cheaper Goods	28
Advertising	30
Railway Servants	32
Accidents: Railway Workers	34
Accidents: The Travelling Public	36
Joining the Union	38
The Unions at Work	40
Railway Relics	42
Biographical Notes	43
The Railway Companies	44
Difficult Words	46
Conversion Table	46
Book List	47
Acknowledgments	47
Index	48

© Sarah Harris 1982
First published 1982

All rights reserved. No part of this publication may be reproduced, in any form or by any means, without permission from the Publisher

Typeset by Tek-Art Ltd, London
and printed in Great Britain by
R.J. Acford, Chichester, Sussex
for the publishers
Batsford Academic and Educational Ltd,
an imprint of B.T. Batsford Ltd,
4 Fitzhardinge Street
London W1H 0AH

ISBN 0 7134 4299 9

Introduction

The railways are such an everyday thing for us that it is very hard to imagine the world before they appeared. It is almost impossible to understand that, in less than fifty years, the landscape was altered, habits of a lifetime were changed, previous notions of time and distance destroyed — all because of the arrival of the railways.

A railway is a combination of an artificial track (the rails) and a mechanical means of pulling loads along it. We know that artificial tracks, often made of wood, have been in existence for many hundreds of years. In the late eighteenth and nineteenth centuries iron rails (tramways) were increasingly developed. These were capable of taking heavier loads. As the iron industry grew, iron was plentiful and becoming cheaper to buy. And, with the rise in manufacturing production, there was a great demand for some way of carrying greater quantities of goods further distances.

For many years horses were used to pull the loads along the iron tramways. During the Napoleonic Wars (1793-1815) horses were in short supply — they were needed in the army — and the pressure was on to find some other way of pulling the wagons. The technical means for producing a moving steam engine had existed since 1782, when James Watt had invented a steam engine that could turn a wheel. Then a Cornish engineer, called Richard Trevithick, succeeded in adapting Watt's idea to a smaller, lighter engine, and in 1804 the first steam locomotive was successfully tested on the Pen-y-Darren Tramroad. The Railway had arrived.

At first, progress was slow, but by 1825 the first "proper" railway, the Stockton and Darlington, was opened. Steam locomotives worked much of its length and offered a new means of transport to the public. By 1860, over 10,000 miles of railway had been constructed. You could travel from Plymouth to Aberdeen, or from London to Holyhead to catch the boat for Ireland. Or you could make less ambitious journeys from a house in the new suburb of Altrincham to your work in Manchester, or from Islip to Bicester on market day. In the market you might find, brought by the railway, fresh fish at a price you could afford. In the cities fresh milk might be available. On Sundays and half-holidays your local railway company might well run an excursion train to a local beauty spot or stately home.

In the early years each new railway was financed, built and controlled by a different company. Some railway companies were very small, such as the London and Greenwich, founded in 1838. Some were large and potentially powerful, like the Great Western Railway (also 1838), which was created to build the railway line from London to Bristol. Before long, however, the smaller lines began to amalgamate (join together), forming such famous companies as the Midland Railway (1844), with its impressive headquarters at Derby and a reputation for providing comfort and care for its passengers. By the end of the century the railway network was dominated by a handful of major companies. These were further reduced to four companies after the First World War, by an Act of Parliament which brought the railways under a degree of public control. The Act required the companies to run the railways in the public interest and to plough back profits in the form of lower fares. After the Second World War the railways were completely nationalized, creating British Rail.

By the time this happened the great days of the railways had been over for some time. Road traffic had been successfully competing for freight since the end of the First World

Useful Sources

War. The private motor car had begun to take passenger traffic. There had been little or no new investment on the railways since the early twentieth century. During the 1950s and early sixties, therefore, the nationalized company undertook major new investment. Steam was abandoned and new diesel and electric locomotives were built; major lines were electrified; and eight thousand miles of railway line were closed.

For many small communities the loss of their railway lines was a severe blow. For rail enthusiasts the end of the steam trains was the end of all that was romantic about the railways. Miles of track, that represented not only years of labour but the lives of men, were pulled up and stations sold off. But the railways of the second half of the twentieth century are still an integral part of Britain's transport system. Passenger trains now travel between London and regional centres at over 100 mph and bulk freight is still carried with economy and speed. Millions of commuters depend upon the railways to take them to work and home again.

This book is not a complete history of the railways. It presents a selection of source material, much of it primary, all of it contemporary, on various aspects of the railways and their development. The extracts have been chosen to give you an idea of the types of material from which historians write their history; to give you an insight into the ideas, experiences and attitudes of the people who lived through the age of the railways or were part of them. They are essentially *selective*, neither giving a complete picture of the topic nor, when put together, the whole history of the railways. But they form a starting point; somewhere where you might begin "Finding Out About Railways".

When you begin to find out about Railways, it's a good idea to have a clear outline of exactly what it is you want to research into. "Railways" is such a vast subject that people will find it hard to be helpful, whereas "The Railway in my Town" or "The Caledonian Railway" would be much more easily dealt with.

When you have decided what you want to do, there are two very important sources of help available to you:

A. *Good modern books on railways* Although these may sometimes be too difficult to read all the way through, they will have at the end a *bibliography*. This will tell you where the author went to find out about railways and where you can look too. A few examples of these books are given on page 47.

B. *The local library* Your local librarian will be able to tell you what sorts of material, similar to the ones mentioned here, are available for you to look at, as well as make other suggestions for you to follow up.

Where to find out about railways

1. PEOPLE

a) *Railway workers* Your local Trades Council, Railway Union Branch or station may be able to put you in touch with someone who worked on the railways in the days of steam and who will be able to give you fascinating information about his working life.

b) *Grandparents* and other older people may well have "railway stories" to tell: about the old companies, when the local branch line was working, or railway outings to the seaside.

2. PLACES

a) *Old railway lines* Details of the sorts of information they can give you are described on page 42.

b) *Your local station* (see page 21) You can often work out interesting information about when the station was built by where it is sited. There might well have been more than one station in your town, in which case it is worth tracing the site of the second one and working out why it was closed.

c) *Museums and railway centres* The National Railway Museum is at York. Locomotives and carriages are preserved there and exhibitions are mounted showing the history of the railways. There are many other smaller museums about the country, e.g. at Swindon, Didcot and Dinting. Some of them are attached to steam-worked railway lines, on which you can take a journey into the past.

3. VISUAL MATERIAL

a) *Old photographs and prints* At many railway museums and railway stations you can find old photographs and prints reproduced as postcards. These cover the old steam locomotives, early carriages and prints of the Navvies building the early railway lines.

b) *Maps* Ordnance Survey maps show the route taken by railways — both those still in use and those now closed down. Some libraries may have a map of your town before the railway came, and it is often interesting to compare the two.

4. WRITTEN SOURCES

a) *Newspapers* Most places had their own local paper in the nineteenth century. These will often contain accounts not only of the opening of the railway but also of the discussions and arguments leading up to it. Accounts of excursions may also be found, and if the paper survived into the 1950s, the closure of local lines made prominent news. Stories of railways will often be found in national newspapers too, especially when accidents occurred.

b) *Magazines* There are a number of railway magazines and journals, e.g. *The Railway Magazine*, dating back to the 1830s, which give detailed information on all aspects of the railways. Some reference libraries contain complete sets of these magazines.

c) *Bradshaw* This was a Railway Guide published annually from 1841 until 1961. It contained all the timetables and many advertisements and gives an excellent impression of the complexities of the railway network.

d) *Advertisements* Look at those in the magazines, newspapers and *Bradshaw*. Some of the best have been reproduced as postcards by the National Railway Museum. They give lots of information about the railways, social customs and people's attitudes.

e) *Memoirs* An increasing number of books have been published recently in which railwaymen recall their working days with steam, and these can provide detailed information not available elsewhere.

f) *Books* A list of contemporary books is given on page 47. There are others you may come across. Many of the railway companies commissioned official histories. These are often extremely tedious to read, but many contain excellent pictures and interesting quotations from documents.

5. STREET, INN AND HOTEL NAMES

These often give useful clues as to when streets were built and where the old railway ran, e.g. Railway View and the Station Arms. The Midland Hotel in Manchester is next door to the now derelict Central Station. Which Railway Company do you think used the Grand Central as its terminus?

The Early Railways

Most of the early tramroads were built as cheap ways for carrying goods from quarries or mines to the nearest canal. But some were built to carry goods back and forth in a local area, and a very small number carried passengers as well. It was the tramroads that carried people which were the real forerunners of the railways we know today.

From the extracts on this page, you can trace the original route of the main line of the Oystermouth Railway on a map. What was the main purpose of the railway originally? What tells you that passenger traffic had become an important source of income by 1816?

THE OYSTERMOUTH RAILWAY

The Oystermouth Railway was started in 1804, and by 1807 it was carrying passengers. To start with, the carriages were improvised from mineral wagons. It was not until 1816 that special covered coaches for passengers were built.

An anonymous traveller left this note of his journey in 1809:

> For the sake of novelty ... we all of us got into the Machine for Oystermouth at 10 o'clock — this vehicle is drawn by one horse and runs upon iron wheels, on the iron railway to the aforesaid village about 5 miles from Swansea — the fare is one shilling.

The new passenger coach, introduced in 1816. What does the design remind you of?

PERMISSION TO BUILD A TRAMROAD

Anyone who wanted to build a tramroad had to receive permission through an Act of Parliament. These Acts were very detailed and can tell us not only where the tramroad was built but also why it was built. For example:

> AN ACT FOR MAKING AND MAINTAINING A RAILWAY OR TRAMROAD FROM THE TOWN OF SWANSEA, INTO THE PARISH OF OYSTERMOUTH IN THE COUNTY OF GLAMORGAN. (29th June 1804)

Whereas the making and maintaining of a Railway or Tramroad for the passage of Wagons and other Carriages, to communicate with the *Swansea* Canal near a certain place called *The Brewery Bank* ... to, or near to, a certain Field called *Castle Hill*, in the Parish of Oystermouth; ... will open a Communication with several extensive Limestone Quarries, Coal Mines, Iron Mines and other Mines, whereby the Carriage and Conveyance of Limestone, Coal, Iron Ore and other Minerals and commodities, will be greatly facilitated, and will materially assist the Agriculture of the County throughout the Line and Neighbourhood thereof, and will in other respects be of great Public Utility; but the same cannot be effected without the Authority of Parliament. And whereas the several Persons herein after named are willing and desirous at their own Expense, to make and maintain the said Railway ... : May it therefore please Your Majesty that it may be enacted ... That the Most Noble *Henry Charles* Duke of *Beaufort*, [and] the Burgesses of the Borough of Swansea, are and shall be united into a Company ... by the Name of *The Oystermouth Railway or Tramroad Company*.

The First Steam Locomotives

RICHARD TREVITHICK'S LOCOMOTIVE

The owner of a Welsh Iron Works, called Mr Homfray, was anxious to obtain a steam locomotive to pull wagons along his tramroad at Pen-y-Darren. He asked a young Cornish engineer, Richard Trevithick, to build him one. Such a wild idea greatly amused Homfray's neighbours, and a friend, Anthony Hill, bet 500 guineas (£525 — a small fortune in those days) that the venture would fail. This is Trevithick's own account of what happened:

> Penydarren February 22 1804
>
> Mr. Giddy,
>   Sir,
>   Yesterday we proceeded on our journey with the engine we carryd ten tons of Iron five waggons and 70 men riding on them the whole of the journey, its above 9 miles which we performed in 4 Hours and 5 Mints. but we had to cutt down som trees and remove some Large rocks out of road the engine while working went near 5 miles pr Hour, there was no water put in to the boiler from the time we started untill we arrived at our journeys end, the coal consumed was 2 Hund^d on our return home abt 4 miles from the shipping place of the Iron, one of the small bolts that fastened the axel to the boiler broak and let all the water out of the boiler which prevented the engine ruturning untill this evening, the Gentleman that bet five Hund^d Guineas against it rid the whole of the journey with us and is satisfyde that he has lost the bet, we shall take forty tons the next journey, the publick untill now called mee a scheming fellow but now their tone is much altered.

GEORGE STEPHENSON

By the late 1820s more and more steam locomotives were being built in engineering works, especially in the north of the country. Perhaps the most famous works was the one belonging to George Stephenson in Newcastle. Some of these early locomotives can be seen preserved in railway museums.

George Stephenson's *Rocket* is probably the most famous early steam locomotive. It could travel at 35 mph. In 1829 an observer wrote about it:

> It seemed indeed to fly, presenting one of the most sublime spectacles of mechanical Ingenuity and human daring that ever the world beheld . . . [it] seemed not to run along the Earth but to fly, as it were, on 'the wings of the wind'.

Read Trevithick's letter to Mr Giddy and make a list of some of the difficulties that engineers would have to overcome before their locomotives could "fly like the wind".

What changes in design can you notice between "Locomotion" and "Auckland"? Why do you think the shape or design of the locomotive changed? What were the engineers trying to do?

No. 1 LOCOMOTION
Built by George Stephenson 1825.
Used to open the Stockton to Darlington Railway, 27th September, 1825.

THE ROYAL GEORGE (1827)
No. 10 AUCKLAND (1839)
Both built by Timothy Hackworth at Shildon, Co. Durham

Building the Railways:

In order to build a railway, a company was first set up. The company raised the necessary money and employed a chief engineer to survey the route, and design and supervise the building of bridges, tunnels, embankments, cuttings and the line itself. The surveys and plans were submitted to Parliament by the company's directors, with other evidence about the need for a railway line.

SURVEYING A RAILWAY LINE

Surveying a line was not always an easy job, as George Stephenson reported to a House of Commons Committee in 1825:

> I believe I was threatened to be ducked in the pond if I proceeded; and of course, we had a great deal of the survey to make by stealth, at a time when the persons were at dinner; we could not get it by night for we were watched day and night, and guns were discharged over the grounds belonging to Captain Bradshaw, to prevent us.

Maidenhead Bridge, built by Isambard Kingdom Brunel, one of the greatest railway engineers.

Engineers and Contractors

DESIGNING A RAILWAY LINE

Railway engineers were designing works on a scale never undertaken before. When we see these works today, we may be impressed by their beauty. But it is important to remember that the greatest achievement of the engineers was not to have designed something beautiful but to have solved great technical problems in their designs.

F.S. Williams was a contemporary historian of the railways. In his book, *Our Iron Roads*, first published in 1852, he described the points the engineer had to take into consideration when designing the bridge over the Thames at Maidenhead:

One of the most remarkable structures of the kind in the country is the bridge which carries the Great Western Line over the Thames at Maidenhead.... Its structure was minutely criticised at the time and many doubts were expressed as to its stability. It was constructed with only two arches because in the middle of the river was a shoal which provided a good foundation and because it was important to keep the deep water free for the navigation. It was also necessary to preserve the gradients of the railway uniform, and this depended upon the height of the arches.

BUILDING THE LINE

Once Parliament had passed an Act allowing a proposed a railway line to be built, the engineer would employ a contractor. The contractor undertook to build the line, under the engineer's supervision, for a *fixed price*. Many contractors went bankrupt, as building the lines often proved more costly than they had thought; but one, in particular, was highly successful. His name was Thomas Brassey (1805-1870).

Sir Arthur Helps, who wrote Thomas Brassey's biography in 1872, lists all the contracts which Brassey won. These are ones he undertook in 1847:

Year	Contract	Partner	Engineer	Agent	Mileage
	Buckinghamshire Railway	. . . .	Mr. Dockray	Mr. S. Horn	47½
	Birkenhead and Chester Junction Railway	. . . .	Mr. Rendel, F.R.S.	Mr. Goodfellow / Mr. Day	17½
	Haughley and Norwich Railway	Mr. Ogilvie	Mr. Locke, M.P., F.R.S.	Mr. P. Ogilvie	33
	Great Northern Railway	. . . .	Mr. J. Cubitt	Mr. Bartlett / Mr. Milroy / Mr. Ballard	75½
1847	North Staffordshire Railway	. . . .	Mr. R. Stephenson, M.P., F.R.S. / Mr. Bidder	Mr. J. Jones	48
	Shrewsbury Extension Railway	Mr. Mackenzie / Mr. Stephenson	Mr. Robertson	Mr. Meakin	3
	Trent Valley Stations	Mr. Mackenzie / Mr. Stephenson	Mr. Bidder and others	Mr. Holme	—
	Blackwall Extension Railway	Mr. Ogilvie	Mr. Locke, M.P., F.R.S. / Mr. Stanton	Mr. Burt	1½
	Richmond and Windsor Railway	Mr. Ogilvie	Mr. Locke, M.P., F.R.S.	Mr. Evans	16½
	Rouen and Dieppe Railway	Mr. Mackenzie	Mr. Neuman / Mr. Murton	Mr. Benyon / Mr. C. Smith	31

There are two particularly famous names among the engineers Mr Brassey worked with. Can you pick them out?

Not everything always went well, even for Mr Brassey. In 1858 he was contracted to build the Bilbao line in Spain:

The agent telegraphed to Mr Brassey to come immediately as a certain bridge had been washed down. About three hours afterwards another telegram was sent, stating that a large bank was washed away; and next morning, another, stating the rain continued and more damage had been done. Mr Brassey turning to a friend, said, laughingly: 'I think I had better wait until I hear that the rain has ceased, so that when I do go, I may see what is *left* of the works, and estimate all the disasters at once, and so save a second journey.'

Would you have expected the agent's news to disturb Mr Brassey more than it did? Does this piece of evidence give you any clues as to why he was successful?

Building the Railways:

The men who did the work building the railway lines were called *navvies*. They had a reputation for being wild and lawless, but most of what we know about them comes from the writing of those who employed them or observed them and from newspaper reports — not from the men themselves.

ATTITUDES TO THE NAVVIES

Lieutenant Peter Lecount, one of the assistant engineers on the London to Birmingham line, wrote:

> These banditti known in some parts of England by the name of 'Navvies' or Navigators... are generally the terror of the surrounding country.... Possessed of all the daring terror of the smuggler, without any of his redeeming qualities their ferocious behaviour can only be equalled by the brutality of their language.

Henrietta Cresswell watched the Great Northern Line being built through her village — Winchmore Hill — in 1869:

> There had been much fear in the village of annoyance from the horde of Yorkshire and Lincolnshire railwaymen brought in by Firbank, the contractor; but on the whole their conduct was very orderly.... A noticeable figure was 'Dandy Ganger', a big north countryman, decorated with many large mother of pearl buttons and a big silver watch chain. He instantly checked all bad language in the neighbourhood of the doctor's garden.

Navvy on the tramp, Punch *1855. What can you tell about the sort of work the navvy did from the equipment he is carrying? The picture of the navvies at work on the London to Birmingham Line gives you extra clues as to the type of work they did.* ▷

THE DEMAND FOR NAVVIES

When work on one railway was finished, the men tramped off to the next. During the height of railway building in the mid 1840s, they were much in demand. Mr MacKay, who worked for Thomas Brassey, the contractor, noted:

> 1846 — Lancaster and Carlisle, Caledonian, Trent Valley, North Staffordshire, Eastern Union Railways in Construction. Height of the railway mania. Demand for labour excessive.... Beer given to men as well as wages. Look-outs placed on the roads to intercept men tramping and take them to the nearest beershop to be treated and induced to start work.

The Navvies

ACCIDENTS AND DEATH

Accidents were commonplace. Henry Pomfret, a surgeon, prepared a list of those just injured during the building of the first Woodhead tunnel between 1839 and 1845 (The Sheffield, Ashton under Lyne and Manchester Railway). It included:

23 cases of compound fracture, including two fractured skulls
74 simple fractures...
140 serious cases, including burns from blasts, severe contusions, lacerations and dislocations.

Patrick MacGill is one of two navvy poets whose work we know about. He wrote of the death of a navvy in a poem called "Played Out":

> As a bullock falls in the crooked ruts,
>   he fell when the day was o'er,
> The hunger gripping his stinted guts,
>   his body shaken and sore.
> They pulled it out of the ditch in the dark,
>   as a brute is pulled from its lair,
> The corpse of a navvy, stiff and stark,
>   with the clay on its face and hair.

△
Navvies at work on the London to Birmingham Line, 1837.

Why do you think the navvies gained a bad reputation? Do you think it was deserved?

11

Opposition to the Railways

The railways are so much part of our world today that we take them for granted. However, they were not universally welcomed when the network first spread across Britain. How would you describe the three different interest groups quoted here and their different attitudes? Which group do you think had the most to lose?

LANDOWNERS AGAINST THE RAILWAY

This petition was published in *The Railway Magazine* in January 1839:

> RAILWAY from STONE to RUGBY — We, the undersigned OWNERS and OCCUPIERS of LANDS on the projected LINE of RAILWAY from STONE to RUGBY, *do hereby declare* our DISSENT from the scheme, and that our determination to OPPOSE it by every means in our power remains unaltered, convinced that it is an unjustifiable interference with and invasion of PRIVATE Property, being wholly uncalled for and unnecessary for the accommodation of the public.
> December 1838   (about 600 signatures)

COACHMEN AND TRANSPORT WORKERS AGAINST THE RAILWAY

In October 1839 this petition was presented to Parliament:

> To the Rt. Hon of the House of Commons in the present Parliament assembled: The Humble Petition of the Coachmen, Hostlers, Helpers, Cads, Cab-drivers, Watermen, and others,
> Sheweth, — That whereas certain favourites of Plutus, affected to the trade and prosperity of this kingdom, taking upon them the name and title of *Railway Projectors and Constructors*, have presumed to secure to her Majesty's subjects in these realms safe and expiditious means of locomotion .... We beg leave humbly to submit to your honourable House —
> That such establishments or institutions are utterly repugnant to well established and respectable customs, and at complete variance with the practices derived from the wisdom of our ancestors, who placed the control and management of the various branches of the art of terrestrial locomotion into the trusty and skilful hands of us, your petitioners.

The railway between Bakewell and Buxton, that Ruskin complained about, is now disused. The abandoned viaduct at Monsal Dale is considered by many to enhance the view at a famous beauty spot. Do you agree?

JOHN RUSKIN AGAINST THE RAILWAY

As the railways ploughed into his beloved Derbyshire, John Ruskin wrote:

> There was a rocky valley between Buxton and Bakewell, once upon a time, divine as the Vale of Tempe; you might have seen the Gods there morning and evening . . . walking in fair procession on the lawns of it. . . . You cared neither for Gods nor grass, but for cash (which you did not know the way to get); you thought you could get it by what the Times calls 'Railroad Enterprise'. You Enterprised a Railroad through the valley — you blasted its rocks away, heaped thousands of tons of shale into its lovely stream. The valley is gone, and the Gods with it; and now, every fool in Buxton can be in Bakewell in half an hour, and every fool in Bakewell in Buxton. . . .
> (*Fors Clavigera*:Letter 5, May 1st 1871)

This came from a series of letters addressed by Ruskin to working men, and published for many years after he retired to Brantwood.

The Hidden Cost

When railways were built through the countryside, hills were blasted away and valleys filled in; but when railways passed through villages or towns, it was homes that were demolished. When the railway was to be built across land owned by rich or important people, the Act of Parliament would insist that they received a reasonable amount of money to compensate them for any inconvenience. This was rarely the case when the railway company planned to pull down the homes of the less powerful.

THE SHEFFIELD AND CHESTERFIELD LINE

When the railway was built from Sheffield to Chesterfield, the Act of Parliament allowed the company to obtain by compulsory purchase:

> 1,061 houses occupied by 5,035 persons of the labouring class; no provision is made in the Bill for the same, as no inconvenience is anticipated.

The *Sheffield and Rotherham Independent* noted in July 1866:

A number of cottage houses have been pulled down on the line of the route, and as Dronfield is a thriving place, and other houses have not been built, there is a great outcry for dwellings of this class. Many families are much inconvenienced, and considerable overcrowding is the result.

and again on November 3rd:

... the compulsory removal of so many working men and their families has been the cause of some hardship, which is unfortunately inevitable under the circumstances. Houses to let are very scarce just now in Sheffield, and the rate at which new houses suitable for the working men are being built does not seem nearly commensurate with the demand for them.

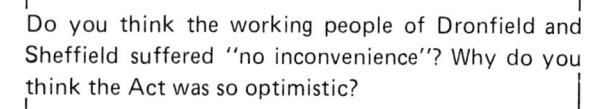

Do you think the working people of Dronfield and Sheffield suffered "no inconvenience"? Why do you think the Act was so optimistic?

◁ *The London and Birmingham Railway cuts through Camden on its way to the terminus at Euston Station, September 1836. This might well have been the scene described by Charles Dickens in his novel,* Dombey and Son:

> The first shock of a great earthquake had, just at that period, rent the whole neighbourhood to its centre. Traces of its course were visible on every side. Houses were knocked down; streets broken through and stopped; ... buildings that were undermined and shaking propped by great beams of wood.

Which of these two pieces of evidence do you think the more reliable, and why?

15

Shareholders

Building a railway cost a great deal of money. No one person could have afforded it, so, in order to raise the money, a company was formed to issue shares which could be bought by anyone with some spare cash. All this money was used to build the railway and, in return, anyone who owned a share would be paid a sum of money, called a dividend, out of any profits that the railway made. The people who had bought shares in the early railways were often paid large dividends and so by the 1840s, everyone who could afford it was eagerly buying shares in any railway scheme that appeared. It was the time of "Railway Mania". The price of shares soared, because everyone wanted to buy them and fortunes could be made.

It soon became clear that some of the companies were not going to be able to pay the high dividends people were expecting. No one wanted their shares any more. People began to sell them and the price began to fall. When it was discovered that one of the most respectable railway businessmen of his day — George Hudson — had been fiddling the books of his company, panic set in and people couldn't get rid of their railway shares fast enough. A number of people lost all their money and went bankrupt.

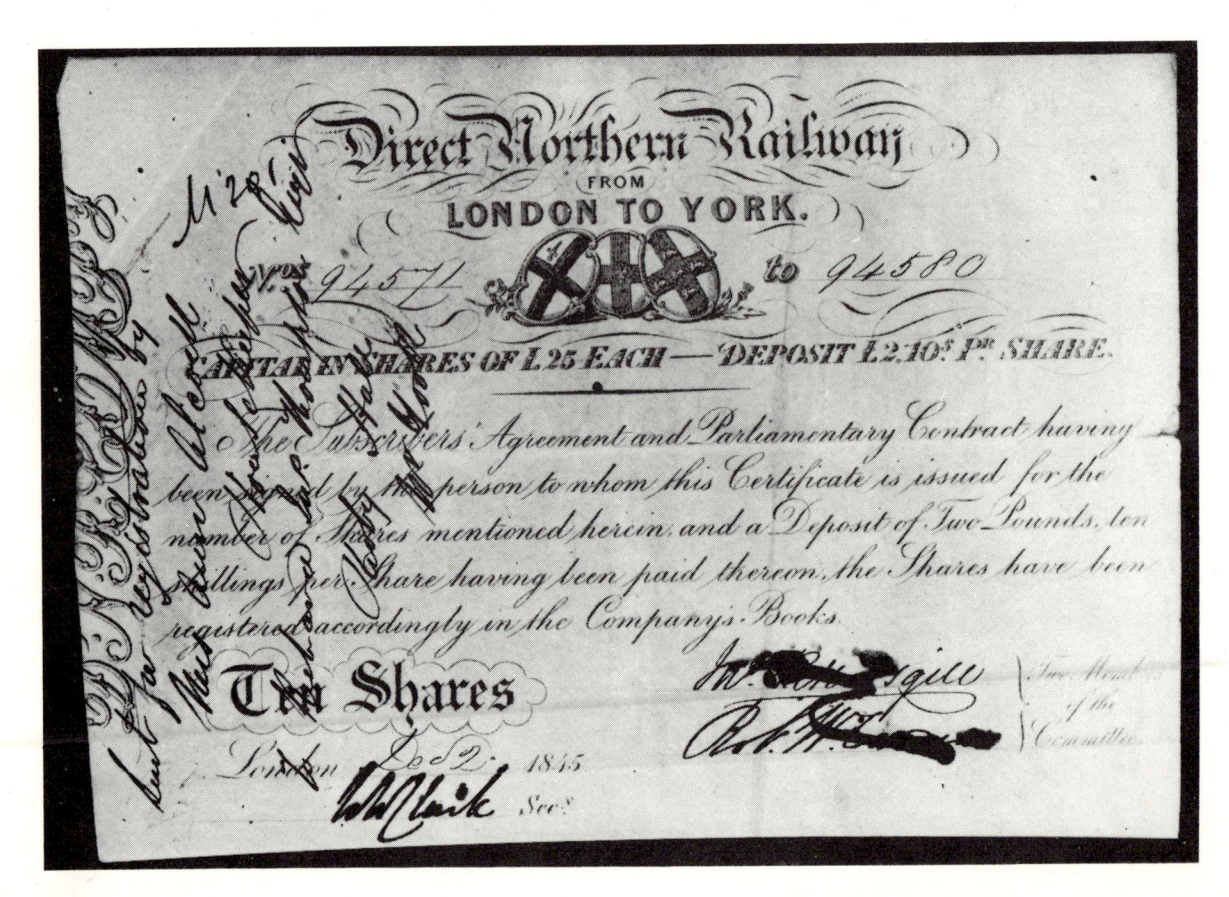

GEORGE HUDSON

In 1849 the *Illustrated London News* tried to explain what had happened:

> But the truth is that Mr. Hudson is neither better nor worse than the morality of 1845. He rose to wealth and importance at an immoral period; he was the creature of an immoral system; he was wafted into fortune upon the wave of a popular mania; he was elevated into the Dictatorship of Railway Speculation in an unwholesome ferment of popular cupidity, pervading all ranks and conditions of men; and whatever be the hue of the error he may have committed, it is rather too much to expect of him that he should be purer than his time or his associates. The commercial code of 1845 was, as far as Railways were concerned, framed upon anything but moral principles. . . . Mr. Hudson, from the superior magnitude of his transactions, from his superior talent in railway business, and perhaps, also, from his superior luck, became the representative of that system. He was to wealth what the Queen is to honour — its fountain; and all who desired to be wealthy without labour, and by a mere turn of the dice of Fortune, looked to him to aid them in their projects.

> Old men and young, the famish'd and the full,
> The rich and poor, widow, and wife, and maid,
> Master and servant -- all, with one intent,
> Rushed on the paper scrip; their eager eyes
> Flashing a fierce unconquerable greed —
> Their hot palms itching — all their being fill'd
> With one desire.

Whatever the morality of the 1840s, it remained true that when the height of activity came to an end, many people of only moderate means held their savings in railway shares, which continued to give them and their heirs a steady income throughout the nineteenth century.

How does the *Illustrated London News* explain "Railway Mania"? Do you think it is a balanced explanation?

EVERY MAN A SHAREHOLDER

In his book, *Our Iron Roads*, F.S. Williams included the following description:

> "Every man of the present day," said Cruikshank in his Table Book, "is a holder of shares in a railway; that is, he has got some pieces of paper called scrip, entitling him to a certain proportionate part of a blue, red or yellow line drawn across a map and designated a railway. . . . Trunk lines are generally the best, because the word trunk connects itself in the mind of the public with the idea of luggage, and a good deal of traffic is consequently relied upon."

◁ *A share certificate.*

Railway Towns

The industrial and agricultural revolutions of the late eighteenth and early nineteenth centuries had already begun to transform Britain from a rural to an urban country. By 1851, half the population lived in towns. The arrival of the railways supported and, in some cases, speeded up these changes. Existing towns could grow with the railways, which brought in food for the people and raw materials for their industries. With quick, cheap travel on the railways, people could live further from the city centre, and so the suburbs grew. Seaside towns expanded to cope with the larger and larger numbers of holiday makers, and new towns were created where the railways set up their large engine workshops.

THE GROWTH OF SWINDON

Swindon, in Wiltshire, was a small market town:

The town is situated on the summit of a hill of considerable eminence, which commands a delightful view of parts of Berkshire and Gloucestershire. The principal streets are wide and contain many good houses. No particular manufacture is carried on in the town, but it is the residence of many persons of independent fortune. Extensive quarries are wrought in the neighbourhood, which, together with agricultural pursuits, afford employment to the greater part of the working population of the town.... There are 325 houses in the town and the population at the 1831 census was 1742. (From *The Parliamentary Gazeteer of England and Wales 1840-1843*)

This picture of New Swindon (looking east) was painted in 1849 by Edward Snell. How many new roads can you identify?

In 1841 the Great Western Railway began building their locomotive works near Swindon. They also built houses for their workers, and the community became known as New Swindon.

The village of New Swindon was GWR property, let exclusively at first to GWR workers. It is interesting to contrast the inhabitants of New and Old Swindon, using the 1851 census returns:

Prospect Place (Old Swindon) 1851

Head of Household	Age	Occupation	Place of Birth
Joseph Miles	34	Cordwainer	Oxfordshire
Henry Coale	29	Currier	Wiltshire
William Hope	29	Cordwainer	Gloucestershire
John Oldland	43	Accountant	Gloucestershire
John Tilby	41	GWR Guard	Wiltshire
Henry Berry	33	GWR Porter	Oxfordshire
Moses Day	40	Stone Mason	Wiltshire
George Wiltshire	29	Stone Mason	Wiltshire
John May	36	Butcher	Wiltshire
Harriet Twiner	50	—	Wiltshire

Bristol Street (New Swindon) 1851

Head of Household	Age	Occupation	Place of Birth
Benjaman Hollows	30	Engine Driver	Lancashire
John Fawcett	33	Engine Smith	Durham
Henry Appleby	49	Engineer	Newcastle
William Hawkins	47	Policeman	Somerset
Augustus Croker	33	Policeman	Wiltshire
Jesse Lockyer	30	Erector	Stroud
John Brown	40	Engine Driver	Durham
John Morrisson	35	Engineer	Scotland
George Thompson	31	Engine Fitter	Scotland
James Holton	29	Smith	Lancashire

Orlando Baker's map of Swindon, 1883. By 1883 Old and New Swindon were creeping together. From the map identify the works, the railway village, the census streets and the church in the picture.

In November 1900, the Borough of Swindon was created, joining together Old and New Swindon.

The Population Growth of Swindon: 1841-1901

Year	New Swindon	Old Swindon	Total
1841	—	2459	2459
1851	2300	2576	4876
1861	4167	2689	6856
1871	7628	4092	11720
1881	15086	4818	19904
1891	27295	5544	32839
1901	—	—	44996

(Home Office Census Returns)

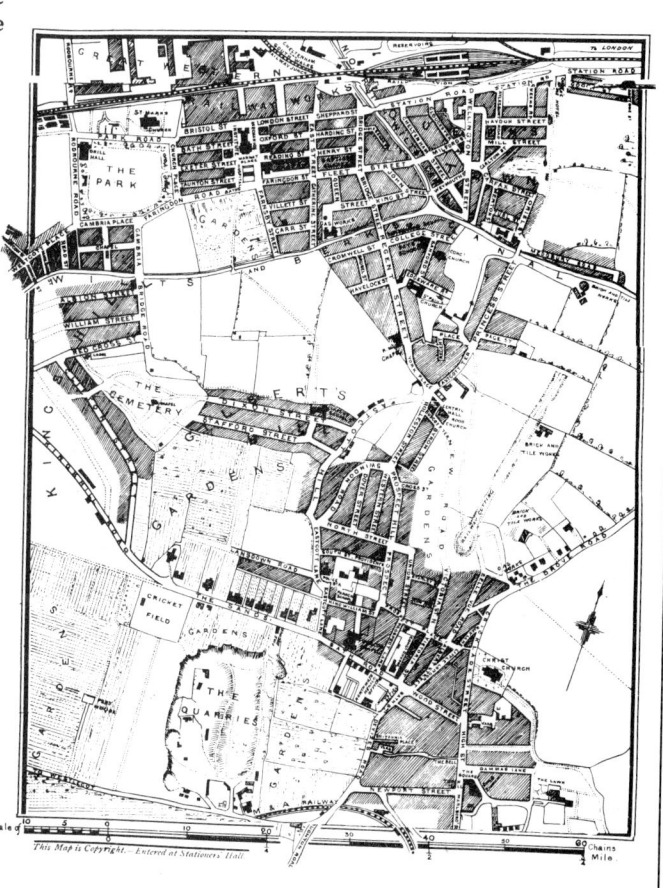

Station Architecture

The station was the place where the railway company met its customers, the travelling public. As a result, and certainly in the early years, great care and enormous sums of money were lavished on the stations, especially the great terminus stations in the big cities. Every style of architecture was represented in the public facades and, inside, the stations were — and many remain today — great cathedrals to Victorian enterprise — chambers of glass and iron. Even quiet country stations often show the careful thought given to the company's public image.

The classic facade of Liverpool Lime Street Station, 1839

THE TERMINUS STATIONS

F.S. Williams wrote in his 1883 edition of *Our Iron Roads*:

> The original cost of the Paddington passenger terminus was £650,000; but for many years the accommodation provided was only 'make shift'. Not till 1854 was the present terminus built. The style is a mixture of Italian and Arabesque; it stands in an area of seventy acres; it has an extreme length of nearly 800 feet; and it is spanned by three semi-elliptical roofs and three transepts. Between the end of the passenger station and the West London junction — a distance of about a mile and a half — there are twelve miles of running lines and thirty-eight miles of sidings. A staff of more than 3,000 officers and men is stationed at Paddington, including the chiefs of the service. Nearly 300 trains pass in or out of the station every day, and about 11,000,000 of passengers every year.
>
> We might describe other metropolitan stations: that at Euston Square, with its Grecian propyleum and stately vestibule; and the Midland at St. Pancras, with its gigantic roof of two and a half acres of glass, 240 feet across, rising 100 feet above the rail level; a station in the construction of which 60,000,000 bricks, 9,000 tons of iron, and 80,000 cubic feet of dressed stone were employed. There is the enlarged station of the London and South Western Company at Waterloo; and the new Liverpool Street terminus of the Great Eastern, that covers ten acres of ground, and has an extreme length of 2,000 feet. There are also the stations at the provincial cities of the great railway companies, where enormous outlay has been incurred. At Manchester, for instance, the London and North Western Company has spent £2,000,000, at Liverpool probably £4,000,000, and at Birmingham £1,500,000, and yet further enlargement has become necessary.

The interior of Charing Cross Station, built in 1864. ▷ Notice the ornate lights and the driveway coming into the station.

20

LOOKING AT YOUR STATION

A number of stations were rebuilt when passenger traffic increased, but often without the imagination and grand vision of an earlier age. Many of the smaller stations have been destroyed, but if your station still exists, take a good look at it. Remember, when it was built, it may well have been on the edge of the town. Passengers would have approached in horsedrawn carriages down a sweeping drive, to enter under an imposing canopy which provided shelter in poor weather. Would it have impressed the prospective customer?

Your local newspaper may have a description of the station when it was opened, like this one from the *Sheffield and Rotherham Independent* on the opening of the Sheffield and Chesterfield Line in 1870:

> The building is of rock-faced wall stone (ashlar from Mexborough) tool dressed; and the style of architecture Grecian with Gothic headings. The roof is of iron and glass, and is supported by forty-two iron columns. The platforms are **700** feet long and thirty feet wide.

Cottage-style station at Woburn, built 1846.

Travelling on the Railways:

The early passenger trains had first class and second class coaches. This reflected the division on stage coaches, of inside and outside passengers, and, as a result, the second class railway coaches were open to the sky. Occasionally, third class passengers were reluctantly carried on the slowest trains, in very poor conditions. It was not until 1844 that an Act of Parliament forced the railway companies to provide at least one train a day for third class passengers, over every line, and laid down that all carriages had to be closed.

A NEW THIRD CLASS CARRIAGE

Eventually, the railway companies were bound to realize that there was a vast, untapped source of passenger traffic among the poorer people. In 1870 the most imaginative of the companies, the Midland Railway, abolished second class travel and introduced a new third class carriage which was attached to all its trains. It had upholstered seats! What do you think was the response of the other railway companies to this new venture by Midland Railway? Look at the picture on page 23.

THIRD CLASS TRAVEL

A railway enthusiast, Samuel Cobham, wrote to the *Railway Magazine* in 1841 about some of his experiences as a third class passenger:

> The 3rd class passengers on most of these lines are subjected to various annoyances; ... they are put in that position in the train where they shall get the most coke-dust, sparks and steam and dirt from the engine; the trains are started at the most inconvenient hours, and so as to get to the terminus at most awkward hours, and generally only once a day: and everything is done to make them as uncomfortable as possible:- their clothes are spoilt and burnt and their persons are burnt also.

Even after 1844 the third class trains didn't go very fast, and third class passengers weren't considered very important.

A second class train on the Liverpool and Manchester Railway, 1831.
▽

The Not So Rich and The Poor

SECOND CLASS TRAVEL

The book, *The Comic Bradshaw* (1848), was a humorous look at railways and railway travellers. Its author, Angus B. Reach, described what it was like to travel in a second class compartment:

> Remarkable Phenomenon in 2nd Class Carriage
> It is a curious fact in connexion with the wood used in the construction of second-class carriages, that the further you travel the harder, and tougher, and rougher, and knottier, do the seats become. At first they seem smooth enough, — in fact, handsome, polished planes. In about thirty miles, they get nutmeg-graterish on the surface; by fifty, lumps begin to grow out of them; by seventy, the lumps are sharper; and ere the hundred be completed, you would exchange your throne for an armchair full of broken bottles.

Interior of the new third class carriage, Midland Railway. ▷

23

Travelling on the Railways:

Class distinctions were carefully preserved on the railways from the earliest days. The rich travelled first class and almost every whim was catered for. *The Comic Bradshaw* (1848) said:

> The 1st class passenger . . . keeps himself to himself. . . . He knows the gentlemen's seats along the line, and the character of the county fox hounds. . . . At stations he asks to see the guard who touches his cap, and says they have thirty-five miles to go.

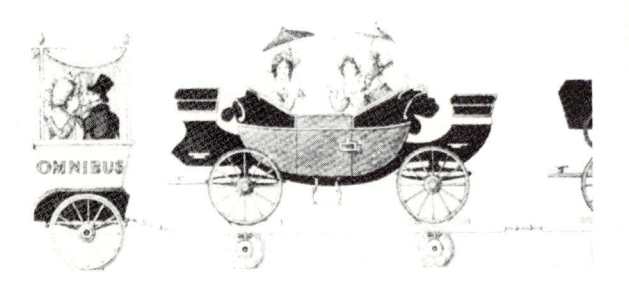

A carriage truck, about 1830.

AVOIDING TRAVELLING WITH STRANGERS

For some very aristocratic people, travelling with complete strangers, even in a closed compartment, was more than they could cope with, and so for many years first class trains included carriage trucks. These enabled the rich to travel in their own carriages.

It was not until **1850** that one family stopped using their own carriage when travelling by train. A.J.C. Hare wrote in his autobiography, *The Years with Mother:*

> At last we came to use the ordinary railway carriage, but then for a long time we used to have post-horses to meet us at some station near London: my mother would not be known to enter London in a railway carriage — 'it was so excessively improper'; so we entered the metropolis by land, as it was called in the early days of railway travelling.

The Rich

A first class train on the Liverpool and Manchester Railway, 1831.

A public drawing room car, similar to the Pullman car described in the extract.

PULLMAN CARS

In 1874 the Midland Railway introduced Pullman Cars from America for their first class passengers. A passenger on the first Pullman train from London to Bedford, in 1874, wrote:

> Literally nothing seemed left to desire. Entering the train from one end, you were introduced to the parlour car, a luxurious contrivance for short lines and day-travel only. It was a tastefully and richly decorated saloon, over fifty feet long, light, warm, well ventilated, and exquisitely carpeted, upholstered, and furnished. Along each side, and close to the windows, were crimson cushioned easy chairs, in which, by means of a pivot you might swing yourself round to converse with your neighbour.

Compare the Pullman car with the original first class carriages. Why might the new carriages have been considered the height of luxury? Why do you think the railway companies went to such lengths to cater for their first class travellers?

A Day Out

From the very earliest days the railway companies offered excursions to the public — a particular train on a particular date for a specific event. It could be to see a cricket match, to visit a stately home or to spend a day at the races. These excursions were often enormously popular, as contemporary newspaper accounts show.

How long did the journey from Canterbury to Victoria take? Was this excursion just for cricket fans?

AN OUTING TO LONDON

The Railway Magazine, 21 September 1841:

We are glad to perceive that railways are becoming more and more useful to society in the formation of excursions of health and pleasure upon a large scale. . . . On Monday last about 850 of the inhabitants of Gloucester, Cheltenham and Cirencester started by a special train . . . to view some of the sights of the modern Babylon. They had previously engaged the train to carry from 800 to 1,000 to London and back for £500; and the expense therefore of the double trip was about 12s each. At half-past ten A.M., they started, and having stopped at many of the stations on the road, partly to see the places, and partly to refect the inward man, the train reached London about 3 p.m. Fast as they had travelled, the news of their approach had reached London before them; and a few 'choice spirits' of the town were waiting to give the 850 Gloucestershire men a hearty reception to the metropolis. One gentleman in deep mourning took his place in a 'bus' filled with some of the jolly looking of the party, and after he had left the omnibus, feeling suddenly unwell, the company found they had lost — one a purse of £5 and another a pocket handkerchief, by the gentleman in the sombre suit.

This excursion took place in 1853. You might like to write an imaginary account of the outing, using the information from the two newspaper accounts to help you. ▷

A VISIT TO THE GREAT EXHIBITION

The Doncaster Chronicle, 6 June 1851:

The first of the Great Northern Excursion Trains ran on Monday. It arrived at Doncaster very punctually and was very full. We emerged from the station drawn by two powerful engines and were soon running a great pace, surrounded by no inconsiderable cloud of dust. At Retford we stopped for ten minutes, to yoke on additional carriages. We were reclining quietly in one of the last carriages when suddenly arose a shout "Stop her," "Stop her!", "She'll be into them!" In great alarm we rushed to the window and beheld a gigantic carriage, laden with Sheffielders, loose from its train, and, bearing slowly down a siding upon the flank of our line. But four sturdy porters flew to the rescue, applied their shoulders with frantic determination to the sluggish mass and another minute saw us relieved of danger. . . . About ten miles from Boston our pace became very slow, and a rumour passed down the train that one of the engines was broken. Soon we came to a standstill. "Here's a pretty fix", said some. "Now, if we have to walk to Boston", said others. Visions of pursuing coal-trains and all manner of disasters floated before our eyes. However there was a movement before long. The lame engine was detached, and we went merrily with the remaining one, indeed there was no perceptible difference in the speed. . . . At Boston we put on another engine and made up time to Peterbro', where the refreshment-rooms and lunch were awaiting us. The arrangements here were admirable, not-withstanding the besieging crowds. . . . "Cup of tea" — "Run please" — pop, pop went the bitter beer bottles — "sixpence, sir" — pop, pop, pop — "Where's my change?" — "Coffee" — "Tea" — pop, pop, — kept up a rapid fire for nearly ten minutes, when the room thinned and the bell rang. As the train left the station a man stood on the step of the carriage, with a bottle in his hand; he jumped off, the train being already in motion, and by the impetus was thrown flat upon his face, and the bottle smashed to atoms. He got up and with a bleeding face tottered into the station. We arrived at London very punctually.

OXFORD, WORCESTER, AND WOLVERHAMPTON RAILWAY.

EXCURSION
At Reduced Fares,
FROM EVESHAM TO
BLENHEIM,
THE SEAT OF THE DUKE OF MARLBOROUGH.

ON WEDNESDAY NEXT, THE 22nd JUNE,

Tickets, at Reduced Fares, will be issued by the Train leaving Worcester at 7.30 a.m., Returning from the Handborough Station (within 2 Miles of Blenheim) at 6.50 p.m. A number of Conveyances will be provided at the Station.

An early application for Tickets should be made as only a limited number will be issued.

Fares to Handborough and Back:
FIRST CLASS — **6s. 6d.**   SECOND CLASS — **4s. 6d.**

By Order, W. T. ADCOCK.

JUNE 16th, 1853.

Cheaper Goods

Railways had been seen originally as a quick, cheap and efficient way of carrying goods from mines to canals, from factories to the sea. Although the railways' success as carriers of people rather than goods was what caught the public imagination, the freight service offered by the railways was of vital importance too.

CARRYING COAL

In 1864 the Vicar of Dore, Mr. J.T.F. Aldred, gave evidence to the House of Commons Committee discussing the building of a railway from Sheffield to Chesterfield. He described the high cost of coal which had to be carried by road.

> Counsel: Do you know that the cost of the carriage of coal has weighed heavily on people in that district?
> Mr. Aldred: Yes, very heavily indeed.
> Counsel: Though they are close to the coalfields, they have to pay a large price for coal?
> Mr. Aldred: In the district in which I live, although we are within four miles of the coal pit, we pay 10s and 12s a ton, the road being so heavy and so uneasy.
> Counsel: And that presses more hardly on people in poor circumstances than it does on persons in your position?
> Mr. Aldred: Yes.
> Counsel: What should you say would be the saving on coal?
> Mr. Aldred: In the district I speak of, I should say that the saving in the carriage alone would amount to £4,000.

SURREY Iron Railway.

The COMMITTEE of the SURREY IRON RAILWAY COMPANY,

HEREBY, GIVE NOTICE,. That the BASON at *Wandsworth*, and the Railway therefrom up to *Croydon* and *Carshalton*, is now open for the Use of the Public, on Payment of the following Tolls, viz.

For all Coals entering into or going out of their Bason at Wandsworth,	per Chaldron,	3d.
For all other Goods entering into or going out of their Bason at Wandsworth	per Ton,	3d.

For all GOODS carried on the said RAILWAY, as follows, viz.

For Dung,	per Ton, per Mile,	1d.
For Lime, and all Manures, (except Dung,) Lime-stone, Chalk, Clay, Breeze, Ashes, Sand, Bricks, Stone, Flints, and Fuller's Earth,	per Ton, per Mile,	2d.
For Coals,	per Chald. per Mile,	3d.
And, For all other Goods,	per Ton, per Mile,	3d.

By ORDER of the COMMITTEE,
W. B. LUTTLY,
Clerk of the Company.

Wandsworth, June 1, 1804.

BROOKE, PRINTER, No. 35, PATERNOSTER-ROW, LONDON.

The Surrey Iron Railway, a tramroad built from Wandsworth to Croydon in 1803, and using horse-drawn trains, was the first line to offer a freight-carrying service to the public.

Early goods trains on the Liverpool and Manchester Railway. These pictures show not only the variety of freight that the railways could carry, but also the quantity that could be carried on a single train. This meant that goods could be carried across the country at a much lower cost.

NORTH EASTERN RAILWAY.
NORTHERN DIVISION.
FISH TRAFFIC
A SPECIAL TRAIN
Will, on and after Monday, August, 1st,

Commence to Run Daily (Sundays excepted) in connection with Trains from York and Normanton to London, Manchester, Derby, Birmingham, Nottingham, &c., and will continue during the Herring Fishing Season or until further Notice.

The following times will be adhered to as far as practicable:—

Leave BERWICK	11. 0 A.M.	Arr. at NEWCASTLE	2.10 P.M.
BEAL	11.18 "	Leave NEWCASTLE	3.10 "
CHATHILL	12. 0 "	Arr at DARLINGTON	5.10 "
CHRISTON BANK	12.15 P.M.	Leave DARLINGTON	5.35 "
LONGHOUTON	12.28 "	" THIRSK	6.35 "
BILTON	12.40 "	Arr. at YORK	7.40 "
ACKLINGTON	12.55 "		

Should it happen that this Train is unable to take Wagons from any of the intermediate Stations named above, the Fish so left will be forwarded, as soon after as Arrangements can be made, by the Ordinary Goods Trains or other Trains as the circumstances may require and will permit.

It must be distinctly understood that, while every effort will be used to insure punctuality, this Company does not undertake that the connection with other Companies' Trains will be at all times maintained, nor do they guarantee the arrival of Fish, (by whatever description of Train forwarded,) at a particular time or for any particular Market.

Fish intended to be forwarded must be delivered at the Stations at least ONE HOUR before the time specified for the starting of the Trains.

Every Separate Package of Fish must bear a FULL and LEGIBLE ADDRESS. The Station Clerks have Instructions to refuse Fish in all Cases in which this Rule is not complied with.

ROBT. PAULING, Goods Manager.
North Eastern Railway Company's Office, Newcastle-on-Tyne, July 23rd, 1864.

Printed by JOHN BELL, Railway Bank Printing Offices, Pilgrim Street, Newcastle-on-Tyne.

△
Fish notice from York.

CARRYING FISH

The *Illustrated London News*, 5 July 1851:

> The railway facilities for conveyance of fish were illustrated on Friday week, in the Committee of the House of Lords on the bill of the Great Northern Railway Company for communication with Grimsby Harbour, by the statement of an extensive dealer in the London Fish-market, that, by means of the railway communication between London and Grimsby, he had received 8,000 Lobsters that morning, and sold them for the supply of the metropolis, the cargo leaving Grimsby at 8 p.m. and arriving in London at 4 a.m.

What would have been the effect of this on the price of lobster in London? What other goods and foodstuffs do you think would have become more easily available as a result of the growing railway network?

Advertising

From the very earliest days the railway companies advertised the routes that passengers could take, and the services and benefits of travelling by railway. Many of the earliest advertisements were full of detailed information, including a time-table of the trains, but by the end of the nineteenth century advertising was becoming more and more sophisticated. The railway companies sometimes employed well-known artists to paint the scenes used in their advertising, and the final posters often contained little or no writing, apart, perhaps, from the name of the town and the initials of the railway company. Posters designed to appeal to particular groups of travellers have always formed a central part of railway advertising too.

What groups of travellers are the advertisements here aimed at? In what ways do they try to achieve an effect? Which do you think the most successful, and why?

If you look at modern railway advertisements, you can discover a great deal about the types of passenger traffic British Rail seeks to attract. Has the emphasis changed at all? If so, why do you think this has happened?

△
Southern Railways, 1936.

◁ *Great Western Railway, 1912.*

This is one of the very earliest advertisements of the ▷ *GWR train service from London to Maidenhead, published in 1839. It is possible to gain an enormous amount of information about early train services from this type of advertisement. What strikes you in particular?*

Great Western Railway.

LONDON TO MAIDENHEAD.

On and after the 1st of May, the SOUTHALL STATION will be opened
For Passengers and Parcels.

An **Extra Train** to Slough will leave Paddington on Sunday Mornings, at half-past 9 o'clock, calling at Ealing, Hanwell, Southall and West Drayton.

Horses and Carriages, being at the Paddington or Maidenhead Station ten minutes before the departure of a Train, will be conveyed upon this Railway.

Charge for 4-wheel Carriage, 12s. Two-wheel ditto, 8s. For 1 Horse, 10s. Pair of Horses, 16s.

Post Horses are kept in readiness both at Paddington and Maidenhead, and upon sufficient notice being given at Paddington, or at the Bell and Mouth Office, St. Martin's-le-Grand, would be sent to bring Carriages from any part of London to the station, at a moderate charge.

TRAINS.

From Paddington	To Maidenhead.	From Maidenhead	To Paddington.
8 o'clock morn. calling at	Southall and Slough	6 o'clock morning, calling at	Slough
9 do.	Slough	7 do. (and on Wednesday Morning at Southall)	Slough and West Drayton
10 do.	West Drayton and Slough	8 do.	Slough and West Drayton
12 do.	West Drayton and Slough	9 do.	Slough and West Drayton
2 o'clock afternoon	West Drayton and Slough	10 do.	Slough and Southall
4 do.	Slough	12 do.	Slough and West Drayton
5 do.	Hanwell and Slough	2 o'clock afternoon	Slough and Southall
6 o'clock evening	Ealing, West Drayton and Slough	4 do.	Slough
7 do.	Southall and Slough	5 do.	Slough and Hanwell
8 do.	Slough	6 o'clock evening	Slough and West Drayton
		7 do.	Slough and Ealing

The six o'clock up Train will call at Southall on Wednesday mornings, for the convenience of persons attending the market on that day.

SHORT TRAINS.

From Paddington To West Drayton.		From West Drayton To Paddington.	
½ past 9 o'Clock Morning,	calling at Ealing, Hanwell, AND Southall.	½ before 9 o'Clock Morning,	calling at Southall, Hanwell, AND Ealing.
½ past 1 do. Afternoon,		½ before 11 do.	
½ past 4 do. do.		½ before 3 Afternoon	
½ past 8 do. Evening		½ before 7 o'Clock Evening	

☞ *There are no second class close carriages in the short Trains.*

Passengers and Parcels for Slough and Maidenhead will be conveyed from all the stations by means of the short Trains, waiting to be taken on by the succeeding long Train, as above; and in like manner they will be conveyed from Maidenhead and Slough, to every station on the Line.

On SUNDAYS.

From Paddington	To Maidenhead.	From Maidenhead	To Paddington.
8 o'clock Morn, calling at	Ealing and Slough	6 o'clock morn, calling at	Slough
½ past 8 do. do.	West Drayton and Slough	8 do.	Slough Southall and Ealing
9 do. do.	Southall and Slough	9 do. do.	Slough West Drayton and Hanwell
5 afternoon do.	Hanwell West Drayton and Slough	5 afternoon do.	Slough
6 evening do.	Ealing West Drayton and Slough	6 evening do.	Slough and West Drayton
7 do. do.	Southall and Slough		Slough and Ealing

SHORT TRAINS,
PADDINGTON TO SLOUGH.
Half-past Nine o'Clock Morning, — — — calling at Ealing, Hanwell, Southall, and Drayton.

To West Drayton.		From West Drayton.	
½ past 9 o'Clock Morning, calling at	Ealing, Hanwell, & Southall. and proceeding to Slough	½ before 8 o'Clock Morning,	calling at Southall, Hanwell & Ealing.
½ past 8 do. Evening,	Ealing, Hanwell & Southall	½ before 7 do. Evening,	

FARES.

Paddington.	1st. Class.	Second Class.		Maidenhead.	1st. Class.	Second Class.	
	Coach.	Close.	Open.		Coach.	Close.	Open.
To Ealing	1 6	1 0	0 9	To Slough	2 0	1 6	1 0
Hanwell	2 0	1 6	1 0	West Drayton	3 0	2 6	2 0
Southall	2 6	1 9	1 3	Southall	4 0	3 0	2 6
West Drayton	3 6	2 0	1 6	Hanwell	4 6	3 6	3 0
Slough	4 6	3 0	2 6	Ealing	5 0	4 0	3 6
Maidenhead	5 6	4 0	3 6	Paddington	5 6	4 0	3 6

The same Fares will be charged from Slough to West Drayton as from Maidenhead to Slough.

OMNIBUSES and Coaches start from Princes Street, Bank, one hour before the departure of each Train, calling at the Angel Inn, Islington; Bull Inn, Holborn; Moore's Green Man and Still, Oxford Street; Golden Cross, Charing Cross; Chaplin's **Universal Office**, Regent Circus; and Gloucester Warehouse, Oxford Street; to the Paddington station.—**Fare 6d.** without **Luggage.**

Railway Servants

Being a railway worker, or "servant" as they were called, was considered a good job in Victorian times. It offered relatively secure employment and a reasonable wage, and many companies set up medical and pension funds for their workers. Because many of the people employed by railway companies came into contact with the public, the companies adopted a policy early on of providing their employees with a distinctive uniform — a new departure at the time. This probably helped in giving a sense of identity to the workers. On the other hand, the companies were no kinder employers than others of their age, and working for the railways and living in railway towns meant being subjected to a harsh discipline.

Station staff at York (North Eastern Railway) in 1909. Can you identify the Station Master? The Minutes of the GWR Directors' meeting and the photograph can tell you something about the hierarchy of railway employees. What clues do they give you?

GWR UNIFORMS

Minutes of the Directors' Meeting, Great Western Railway, May 1838:

> Upon consideration of the Livery, IT WAS RESOLVED
> That the Coats and Waistcoats be made of dark rifle green edged with scarlet of the patterns now chosen.
> That the trowsers be made of dark Oxford mixture of the pattern also chosen.
> That the Buttons be gilt and of the size now exhibited as a Pattern.
> That the Inspector of Police be distinguished by a red stripe of an inch and a quarter on the Trowsers.
> That the Sub-Inspectors be marked by an edging on the Trowsers of the same width as the edging of the Coat.
> That the Policemen have G.W.R. with a number marked on the stand-up collar in scarlet cloth.
> That the Hats of the Policemen be precisely similar to those of the Metropolitan Police.
> That the Conductor be required to wear a small Badge on the button hole of his Coat with the Buttons of G.W.R., not having any Livery.
> That the Guards have a Frock Coat and Waistcoat with G.W.R. on the fall of the Collar.
> Trowsers of Oxford Mixture plain.
> The boys to have a common close jacket with Trowsers.
> The Porters to have sleeved Jackets with G.W.R. painted on the Glazed Hats and a badge with G.W.R. and a number on the arm.

MECHANICS INSTITUTE, SWINDON

Dores Swindon Almanack and Public Register gives an example of the positive side of working for the railways. It describes the Mechanics Institute in Swindon New Town, supported, built and paid for by the GWR:

> ... founded in 1843, it now numbers upwards of **600** members. The noble building of the Institution was opened in 1855. The library contains upwards of 3570 volumes comprising a large number of standard works of fiction, and many valuable works on Science, History, Biography etc. **(1864)**

RULES AND REGULATIONS

1877: North Eastern Railway, General Rules and Regulations:

Any workman creating tumult or noise in the works at any time, to be fined___*1s 0d*
Any workman taking strangers into any of the works without leave, or talking to such as may go in to be fined_____*6d*
Washing the hands in oil or otherwise washing or making an improper use of it_____*1s 0d*

Notice to Foreman and Workmen from the Manager, Swindon Works, 10 November 1859:

NOTICE

It having come to my knowledge that many of the boys of New Swindon are very unruly and mischievous in their conduct, especially during the evening when property is frequently damaged and, (as on a recent occasion) life endangered, I hereby give notice that any person in the service of the company reported to me as being disorderly, firing Cannon, or making an improper use of Firearms in the Village be discharged, and as the Parents in most cases are to blame for not checking such bad conduct amongst their children, I consider it my duty for the protection of the Inhabitants and the Company's property to hold the Workmen in the Factory responsible for the behaviour of their children, and shall not hesitate to discharge any man who allows any of his family to commit such offences.

What do you suppose the children were up to? Do you think such a notice would be effective? Do you think it "fair"?

Accidents:

Being a railway worker was a fairly dangerous job for some considerable time after the railways were first built. How dangerous can be discovered by examining the reports of the Amalgamated Society of Railway Servants (ASRS), founded in 1871.

WORKERS KILLED AND INJURED, 1874

The ASRS published the following table in a booklet called "An Appeal to Parliament and Public". They hoped to persuade Parliament to do something to make working and travelling on the railways safer.

Proportion of Killed or Injured During the Year 1874

	GNR 1 in every	GWR 1 in every	MS & LR 1 in every	LNWR 1 in every	NER 1 in every	LYR 1 in every	MR 1 in every
Of Engine-drivers	71 employed	95 employed	151 employed	71 employed	7 employed	15 employed	129 employed
Firemen	71 "	49 "	53 "	54 "	23 "	11 "	503 "
Passenger Guards	56 "	41 "	11 "	28 "	8 "	9 "	49 "
Goods Guards	28 "	13 "	9 "	16 "	8 "	4 "	49 "
Shunters	43 "	22 "	8 "	13 "	25 "	14 "	18 "
Porters	101 "	34 "	100 "	85 "	35 "	18 "	418 "

RECORDS OF ACCIDENTS

ASRS Executive Report, June 1878:

Superannuation [pension] for Accident: The following claims were granted under this head:-
SHAW — Miles Platting Branch
KICK — Aberdare Branch
HARDING — Paddington Branch
FORD — Northampton Branch

From the ASRS General Secretary's Report, July 1878:

Claims to be decided by the AGM:
For Accident:
George Chivers aged 55 of Kings Cross Branch, Shunter on Great Northern Railway. Joined January 1873. In May 1874, he was caught between the coupling of two wagons, and his chest was crushed. The injuries eventually compelled him to give up work. The medical examiner says the claimant is permanently disabled from any kind of work.

This table is quite a good example of how misleading "official" statistics can be. As the ASRS pointed out in their document, the LYR appear to have a very bad record of safety, but these figures are based on each company's own returns and whereas the LYR was conscientious in reporting all accidents, many of the others failed to report the "less serious" ones. Using the figures in the table, work out which was the most dangerous occupation and which the safest. Can you think of any explanation for your answers?

Accidents to servants are still on the increase. During 1877, 684 servants were killed and 3,954 injured, as against 696 killed and 3,872 injured in 1876. Little, indeed, has been done to provide for their greater safety. (ASRS General Secretary, 1878)

Railway Workers

THE DEATH OF A PLATE-LAYER

Patrick MacGill, the navvy poet, wrote of the death of a plate-layer (a person who laid the railway track) in a poem called "Run Down", published in 1911:

In the grim dead-end he lies, with
    passionless filming eyes,
English Ned, with a hole in his head,
Staring up at the skies.

The Engine driver swore as often he swore
    before —
"I whistled him back from the flamin'
    track,
An' I couldn't do no more."

The gaffer spoke through the 'phone
    "Platelayer Seventy-one
Got killed today on the sixfoot way
By a goods on the city run.

"English Ned was his name
No one knows whence he came,
He didn't take mind of the road behind
And none of us are to blame."

They turned the slap in the bed
To cover the clotted red,
Washed the joints and the crimsoned
    points,
And buried English Ned.

In the drear dead-end he lies
With the earth across his eyes
And a stone to say
How he passed away
To a shift beyond the skies.

Gravestone at Bromsgrove. ▷

Accidents:

The accidents which hit the headlines and got most of the attention were the ones in which passenger trains were involved and where members of the public were killed. Such accidents were often followed by an enquiry, which would make recommendations to improve the safety of rail travel, but these recommendations were often ignored or introduced only slowly and reluctantly by the railway companies. In 1889, after a dreadful accident at Armagh, Parliament took action and forced the railway companies to introduce two long-overdue safety measures: the block system and continuous braking. The block system used the newly invented electric telegraph to pass signals down a line, to make sure that no train entered a section (or block) of line until it was clear. Automatic continuous braking ensured that there was a braking system on all carriages that would work whether or not they were still attached to the engine.

In this accident, the Scottish Express ran into a local train when the system devised for working the signals in fog failed to work properly.

ACCIDENT AT ARMAGH

In the accident at Armagh in 1889, 80 people were killed, many of them small children on a Sunday School outing from Armagh to Warrenpoint.

The *Times*, 13 June 1889:

Sergeant Burkin of the band of the Royal Irish Fusiliers.

'I was in the guard's van next the engine. I heard the guard remark to a comrade, "It's too much for her," meaning the engine. A few minutes later the train came to a standstill and I next saw a portion of the train leaving us and going down the incline, after which I heard someone shout "Cog the wheels". But whatever was done was not sufficient to stop the runaway train, for it seemed to go faster. The guard then shouted "My God, there will be a collision," and almost at the same moment we started in pursuit, but were unable to reach the carriages in front of us. A mile down the incline we heard a crash and as soon as we could stop we did so. When we jumped out we found a fearful accident had happened. On every side bodies were lying, some being frightfully mangled. I gave a hand and soon we had most of the people from underneath the splinters.'

Why do you think it was after this accident that Parliament took action?

The Travelling Public

The Brecon and Merthyr Railway. ▷ Block telegraphing was introduced in 1865. Can you explain in your own words how the system worked? Was it fool-proof, do you think?

BRECON AND MERTHYR SECTION.

Regulations for Working the Line by Block Telegraph.

A Train Ticket is to be carried with each Train, to and fro, without which no Engine or Train is to be allowed to start from a Block Station.

The following are the "Block Stations :"—Brecon. Talyllyn, Talybont, Cyfarthfa Junction, and Dowlais.

After "Line Clear" has been obtained, in accordance with the Regulations as stated below, the Station Master, or person in charge for the time being, will make out and deliver to the Engineman a paper Ticket, authorizing him to proceed to the next Block Station, this Ticket must be given up to the Station Master, or person in charge, upon the Train arriving at the Block Station, and the peg of the Instrument must not be removed, or Line Clear be given, until this Train Ticket has been received.

Regulations for Signalling Trains and for obtaining "Line Clear."

The "Block" or Signal Instruments are to be devoted *exclusively* to Signalling of Trains, and the *authority* to work them is entrusted *solely to the Station Master*, without whose authority no Signal whatever is to be passed.

In order to make these Regulations more clearly intelligible, it is proposed to designate the Station from which the Train is to start as "Station A," the Station to which the Train is to proceed as "Station B."

1—Immediately previous to starting a Train at Station A, the needle must be moved steadily to and fro, so as to call the attention of Station B to which the Train is to proceed.

Station B will repeat the Signal to show his attention has been obtained.

Station A will then give *three steady beats* of his needle to the *right*, signifying '*Is Line Clear ?*'

If Line is Clear Station B will repeat, "*Yes, Clear,*" by *repeating the same number of beats* also to the *right*.

Station A will, on receiving the above reply, signal to Station B, "*Train will start,*" by giving *three steady distinct beats* of his needle to the *left*, upon which Station B will place and block the needle opposite to the words on the dial, "*Train on Line.*"

Station A will start Train as soon as he perceives that Station B has blocked the needle in answer to the signal "*Train will start.*"

Immediately on the Arrival of the Train at Station B the *Peg* is to be removed, and Station A is to be advised of it by giving *one steady beat* of the needle to the *right, which Station A will acknowledge* to Station B in the *same manner.*

2.—If, when the signal is given from Station A "*Is Line Clear ?*" the Line should *not* be clear, the reply "*No, blocked,*" is to be immediately returned by Station B, by giving *eight distinct beats* to the *left*; and the needle at B is then to be *permanently blocked over to the left until the Line is clear,* when the peg is to be removed and the Instrument left free for a repetition of the enquiry.

3.—On receiving the reply at Station A, "*No, blocked,*" it will be the duty of the person in charge of the Instrument at Station A, to watch it until the needle is restored to its normal or "perpendicular" position; and then the question, "*Is Line clear ?*" must be repeated from A to B, and *under no circumstances whatever is the Train to be started* until the *reply* is received at A, "*Yes, Line clear,*" and Station B has in reply to signal "*Train will start,*" blocked his needle over to "*Train on Line.*"

4.—After the signals "*Train will start*" have been given from A to B, and Station B has pegged the needle to the *left* "*Train on Line*," the Instrument is to be carefully watched until the needle is restored to its normal position.

5.—Should anything occur at a Station by which the "*Line is blocked,*" so as to prevent or render dangerous the passing of a coming Train, the Stationmaster on both sides are to be immediately advised thereof by first calling attention, and then giving *eight distinct beats* of the needle to the *left*, and the needle is then to be *blocked* over to "*Train on Line*" until the obstruction has been removed, when the peg is to be taken out, and the needle restored to its normal or "perpendicular" position.

6.—The times at which "*Line clear*" is received, "*Time of departure of Train,*" and time of receipt of signal *Train has arrived,* are to be carefully entered in "*Line Clear Book,*" at the Stations, and the signature of Clerk placed opposite to the entries. The *book always to be left open* in a convenient position near the Instrument.

7.—The Station Master at Station B *must,* at all times, *before he replies* "*Yes, Line clear,*" satisfy *himself* it is free, not only from the *ordinary Trains,* but also from any Special Trains, Ballast Trains, Trucks, or other obstructions, he must also be sure *that no Train has been divided and only part of it brought in to his Station,* as may sometimes happen with *heavy Goods Trains.*

8.—Should the Block Telegraph be out of order, recourse must be had to the Single Needle Telegraph, and the *following rules strictly observed :*

When a Train is ready to leave Station A, the question is to be asked of Station B, "*Is Line clear ?*" Station B will reply, (as the case may be) with "*Yes, Line is clear,*" or "*No, blocked,*" and the *question and answer must be* entered in the Line Clear Book at both Stations. If the answer has been received at Station A that the Line is blocked, the Train must not be started from that Station until another message is received from Station B that "*Line is clear.*" Station A must then send message to Station B "*Train will start,*" and Station B must reply to Station A as soon as it is ascertained that the whole of the Train has arrived. "*Train arrived.*"

Upon no consideration, and under penalty of instant dismissal, must any Person signal "LINE CLEAR," until he has been instructed by the STATION MASTER, or his Deputy to do so.

BY ORDER.

Traffic Manager's Office Brecon, June 1st, 1865.

ACCIDENT NEAR HAMPTON WICK

On Christmas Eve, 1874, part of a GWR train from Oxford to North Wales left the track near Hampton Wick. Thirty-four people died. *The Manchester Guardian* published a list of the unidentified bodies on 26 December, among them:

Midshipman or mate, 30, pipe and tobacco, paper with name of 'Pilkington'

A man, ticket to Dolgelly, third class, two photographs of a woman, German silver watch and chain £4.10s 8d in cash, beard and moustache, age 45

Girl, seven years old

A woman, much bruised, 30, single, 'J. Pearson' on handkerchief.

Joining the Union

From the 1870s a strong trade union organization developed among railway workers. In 1871 the Amalgamated Society of Railway Servants was founded (which became the National Union of Railwaymen in 1913); in 1880 the Associated Society of Locomotive Engineers and Firemen was founded; and in 1897 the Railway Clerks Association (RCA) — now the Transport Salaried Staffs Association. From the extracts here, what do you think are the most powerful arguments for joining a union?

WORKERS COMBINE

Richard Bell, General Secretary, ASRS, 1900:

> Helpless and Hopeless will ever be our lot without combination. To our-selves alone should we look for help, with full confidence in the eternal justice of our cause and the righteousness of our principles.

A LETTER FROM THE MANAGEMENT OF THE MIDLAND RAILWAY

General Manager's Office,
Derby, Dec. 19th 1878

General Order No.307

REDUCTION OF WAGES etc.

The Directors have decided that, on and from January 10th 1879, the Wages of Signalmen and Pointholders in receipt of 17s per week and upwards, shall be reduced one shilling per week; the men's time being computed as at present.

Please communicate this to the men under your supervision and carry out the arrangement, commencing with Pay Bill for week ending January 16th 1879

James Allport,
General Manager

What effect do you think this sort of letter might have had on Union recruitment?

ASRS membership card from the 1870s. John Abbott was a delegate at the original Great Delegate Meeting of 24 June 1872, which really launched the union. What were his union dues? Did he pay regularly?

THE BENEFITS OF UNION MEMBERSHIP

In a recruiting leaflet published in the 1920s, the RCA described the work it did on behalf of its members:

> The functions of the R.C.A. are to maintain the standards which have been won and to improve them when opportunity occurs, both collectively and individually.
>
> The R.C.A. does this because it is the negotiating medium with the Railway Companies on all questions of salary agreements and conditions of service which concern the staff as a whole....
> It provides friendly society benefits to members by way of —
> Retirement Benefit
> Death and Disablement Benefit
> Accident Benefit
> Unemployment Benefit
> Convalescence Benefit...
> The R.C.A. is ourselves and our friends and our fellow workers.

WOMEN IN THE UNIONS

During the First World War the numbers of women in employment rose rapidly, and this was particularly true in the clerical sections of the railways. The RCA undertook well-organized campaigns to recruit the new women workers into their union.

1916: Recruiting Leaflet "To A Lady Clerk" from the RCA General Secretary:

> In conclusion I would once more emphasise that the R.C.A., recognising that
> 'The woman's cause is man's, they rise or sink
> Together, dwarf'd or godlike, bond or free,'
> claims from the Railway Companies equality of treatment for men and women, and by resolution of its Annual Conference has requested the Branches to increase their efforts to organise the women clerks with that object in view.

"ONLY A LOCOMOTIVE FIREMAN"

An anonymous poet, a member of ASLEF, wrote the following poem to explain why he thought Union membership important:

> 'Only a Locomotive Fireman', with shovel and pick in hand,
> Furnishing the steam to whirl millions round the land;
> Through tunnels, over bridges, through blinding snow and rain,
> But the people think him only a fireman on the train...
>
> 'Only a Locomotive Fireman', well, as the days go by,
> We must stand by one another, Shall I tell the reason why?
> 'In Union there is Strength,' and no motto can there be,
> Better for the Associated, or for you and me.
>
> 'Only a Locomotive Fireman', but if true to one another,
> If I to you, and you to me, are as brother to a brother,
> Then 'Only a Locomotive Fireman' in power shall expand,
> Till the people all shall hail it as the proudest title in the land.

39

The Unions at Work

During the last years of the nineteenth century the railway unions became steadily more powerful. They offered the railway workers valuable protection, not only through the friendly society funds but also by successfully defending members accused of causing accidents (when often the fault lay with the company). This ensured a steady growth in membership.

By the twentieth century the unions were strong enough to influence events and demand the right to represent their members in negotiations with the railway companies. In 1906 they began a long campaign for an improved national wage structure and better conditions at work. The ASRS adopted a programme called "The National All Grades Movement" and sought to negotiate their proposals directly with the companies. After a long struggle, which ended in a national rail strike in 1911, the House of Commons forced the companies to enter negotiations with the railway unions. The unions had officially arrived. By the end of the First World War, proper committees had been set up at which the unions could meet their employers and discuss anything that affected the working lives of their members, such as pay and hours of work.

EQUAL PAY

Minutes of meeting at Charing Cross Hotel, 5 August 1920, between Management and Unions:

> The representatives of the Unions stated that they could not accept the scheme submitted by the Standing Committee of General Managers in regard to the rates of pay and conditions of service of Railway Female Clerical Staff . . . and claimed that the work carried out by Female Clerks was comparable with that performed by males and justified equality of treatment . . . .
>
> The Chairman intimated that if the claim was for the male clerks' scale to be adopted for Female Clerical Staff, he was afraid it was out of the question but promised the proposal outlines . . . should be considered.

LOCO MEN'S WORKING DAY

ASRS, General Secretary's Report, 18 June 1900:

> **Lancashire and Yorkshire Railway Loco Men**
> I received complaints from Newton Heath No.1, Liverpool No.1, and Fleetwood Branches that the company was breaking the loco-men's agreement with regard to the ten-hour working day. It seems there are a number of small shunting engines and the men in charge of them were compelled to work eleven hours for the ordinary day's pay. At some of the stations too the firemen provided were youths at 2s 6d per day, whilst at Salford no firemen were provided at all.
>
> I took the matter up with the chief mechanical engineer, and, although I did not receive a reply the arrangement by which the men worked eleven hours for the day's pay has been abolished.

HOURS OF DUTY

Letter from the General Secretary, RCA, to the Secretary, Railways Staffs Conference, April 1926:

Night Duty in Control Office, Swansea, Great Western

The hours of duty in this office have always been 44 per week, but last year a change was made in the basis of payment for overtime, and instead of the men being paid on a 44-hour basis they were then and have since been paid on a 48 hour basis. This practice . . . is entirely wrong, and I should be obliged if you would arrange for the matter to be discussed at our meeting with the Railways Staff Conference.

What is the ASRS trying to say in this cartoon?

Why do you think the matters here were of concern to the unions? What do you think might have been the outcome of the negotiations in each case?

Railway Relics

The closure of thousands of miles of railway lines in the years since the Second World War has left a great deal of archeological remains that most of us can investigate on our own doorsteps. Ordnance Survey maps will show you where the now abandoned railway lines once ran. Some have been turned into public amenities, such as nature trails or adventure playgrounds. Some have now become overgrown and impassable. Many stations and station buildings have been adapted for private use or for use as country centres for schools and other institutions. But if your local old railway line is accessible to the public, a pair of sharp eyes will often reveal fascinating relics of the past.

A discarded railway sleeper, now looking like part of the undergrowth.

The station waiting room from Dunvant Station, on the old Swansea Bay Railway, is now used as a garden shed. The date of its construction is above the door (1874).

On the abutments of the bridge over the River Usk of the now abandoned Abergavenny to Merthyr Tydfil Railway is etched the name of the railway engineer. On the other abutment is the date of construction, 1868.

Driving along in a car it is often possible to identify the great earthworks of the Railway Age — cuttings, escarpments, tunnels, and to spot the bridges and viaducts designed and built over a hundred years ago.

Patrick MacGill wrote in 1911, that when all the navvies were gone . . .

> Perhaps some mortal in speaking will give us a kindly thought —
> 'There is a muckpile they shifted, here is a place where they wrought',
> But maybe our straining and striving and singing will go for nought.

Biographical Notes

BRASSEY Thomas (1805-1870) b. Aldford, Cheshire. Educated in Chester and then articled to a land surveyor. Met George Stephenson in 1834 and through him contracted to build the Penkridge Viaduct on the Grand Junction Line. Stephenson's pupil, Locke, took over as chief engineer on this line, and in Locke's subsequent employment he often sought Brassey as his contractor. Brassey was an excellent organizer, good at delegation and popular with his workers. He built thousands of miles of railway lines at home and abroad. m. 1831 3c

BRUNEL Isambard Kingdom (1806-1870) b. Portsmouth. Educated privately and at Henri IV College, Paris, famous for its mathematics teaching. Worked for his father at first (also an engineer). Designed the Clifton Suspension Bridge, begun in 1836. In 1833, was appointed Engineer to the Great Western Railway. His last, and greatest, railway work was the Royal Albert Bridge, crossing the Tamar at Saltash. Designed ocean-going steam ships, such as the Great Britain (1845). m. 1836 3c

HUDSON George (1800-1871) b. near York. Served his apprenticeship as a draper. 1837 Lord Mayor of York. Founded the Yorkshire Bank. Invested his capital in railways and in 1837 became chairman of the Yorkshire and North Midland Railway. Took on other chairmanships, including the Midland Railway, which he created from amalgamations. MP for Sunderland 1845. After the fall in the price of railway shares (1847) was forced to resign his chairmanships, and it was discovered he was in debt to many of his own companies. m. 1828

LOCKE Joseph (1805-1860) b. Sheffield. Educated at Barnsley Grammar School. In 1823 articled to George Stephenson in Newcastle. Helped build the Manchester and Liverpool Railway. Gained a reputation for building railway lines cheaply because he was prepared to use steeper gradients and therefore avoided expensive tunnels etc. Designed the "Crewe" Engine where the parts were so precisely engineered that they could be fitted to any engine of the same design. 1847-1860 MP for Honiton. m. 1834

MACGILL Patrick (1890-197?) b. Ulster. One of six children. Left school at 12 and hired himself out as a farm labourer. Hated being bound to his employer. Left for Scotland in 1904 and became a navvy in 1908. Published *Gleanings from a Navvy's Scrapbook* (poems) 1910; *Songs of a Navvy* 1912; *Children of the Dead End* (autobiography) 1914 and subsequent novels. m. Margaret Gibbons.

STEPHENSON George (1781-1848) b. near Newcastle. First employment herding cows. Then worked in a colliery when he began going to night school to learn to read and write. Was promoted to be in charge of the engines at the colliery as he showed such skill in dealing with them. Built his first steam locomotive in 1814. Designed the tracks for his locomotives to be as level as possible. Was appointed engineer to the proposed Stockton and Darlington Line in 1821. Set up an engineering works in Newcastle to build the locomotives for his line. The first locomotives on the Stockton and Darlington line travelled at 12-16 mph. Founded the Institution of Mechanical Engineers. m. 1802 1c (Robert)

STEPHENSON Robert (1803-1859) b. Newcastle. Educated at schools and Edinburgh University. Assistant to his father. Many of the improved design features on the *Rocket* were due to him. 1833 was appointed engineer on the London and Birmingham Railway, which established his reputation as a great engineer. Engaged in railway building all over the world. The most famous of his works were his bridges, including the Menai Rail Bridge and the Victoria Bridge over the St Lawrence at Montreal. 1847-1859 MP for Whitby. m. 1829

TREVITHICK Richard (1771-1833) b. Cornwall. Unpopular with his schoolmaster but good at arithmetic. A very powerful wrestler. By 1796 was making model steam locomotives. 1804 built the locomotive for the Pen-y-Darren tramroad. 1808 built the "Catch-me-who-can" which ran on a circular railway in what is now Euston Square. The enterprise collapsed when a rail broke and the locomotive left the line. He died in debt but his work-mates clubbed together to give the "great inventor" a decent funeral. m. 1797 6c

The Railway Companies

This is a list of some of the most famous railway companies, with their initials and dates of opening. Those marked with an asterisk were primarily amalgamations of already existing lines.

BR	British Rail* (The Nationalized Company)	1948
CR	Caledonian Railway	1848
ECR	Eastern Counties Railway	1836
GJR	Grand Junction Railway	1837
GNR	Great Northern Railway	1850
GWR	Great Western Railway	1838
LYR	Lancashire and Yorkshire Railway*	1847
L & MR	Liverpool and Manchester Railway	1830
L & BR	London and Birmingham Railway	1838
L & BR	London and Brighton Railway	1841
LCDR	London, Chatham and Dover Railway	1860
LNWR	London and North Western Railway*	1846
L & SR	London and Southampton Railway	1839
LSWR	London and South Western Railway	1840
MS & LR	Manchester, Sheffield and Lincoln Railway	1846
MR	Midland Railway*	1844
NER	North Eastern Railway*	1854
SER	South Eastern Railway	1844
S & DR	Stockton and Darlington Railway	1825

Railway Company badges.

Railways in England and Wales 1847

Key to Major Railways
1 ECR
2 GWR
3 LYR
4 L & BR
5 LNWR
6 LSWR
7 MS & LR
8 MR
9 SER
10 S & DR

In 1921 an Act of Parliament reduced the number of Railway Companies operating the network to four. They were:

LMS — London Midland and Scottish Railway. 7,525 miles long, serving North West Britain. Its engines and carriages were "crimson lake".

LNER — London and North Eastern Railway. 6,714 miles long, serving North East Britain. Its engines were apple green and its carriages teak.

GWR — Great Western Railway. 3,795 miles, serving South Wales, South West England and parts of the Midlands. Its engines were Brunswick green and its carriages chocolate and cream.

SR — Southern Railway. 2,198 miles, serving Southern England. Its engines and carriages were sage green.

Difficult Words

cab-driver	driver of a one-horse public carriage
cad	a conductor on a horse-drawn omnibus
commensurate	equal
commodities	goods
cordwainer	shoe-maker
cupidity	greed
currier	leather worker
dead-end	the end of a railway track, at a siding
expeditious	speedy
favourites of Plutus	wealthy people
fireman	the person who maintained the fire in the boiler of the steam locomotive
gradient	slope
helper	a groom's assistant
hostler	a stable-man or groom
hund^d	hundred (in the case of coal, hundredweight)
loco-man	a railway worker employed on the locomotive itself
metropolis	city, usually London
propyleum	gateway
refect	to refresh with food and drink
scrip	share certificate
shunter	a person employed to move trains from the main line to a siding and back
superannuation	pension
Tempe	a beautiful valley in Greece. The Romans used the word to describe any lovely place
terrestrial	earth-bound
waterman	a boatman who plies for hire on a river or canal

You should be able to find the meaning of any other difficult words in a dictionary

CONVERSION TABLE

NEW MONEY		OLD MONEY
1p	=	2.4d
5p	=	1s. (1 shilling)
50p	=	10s. (10 shillings)
£1	=	£1
		12d = 1 shilling
		20 shillings = £1

Book List

These are some contemporary books about railways, which you might well be able to find in your local reference library:

'Bradshaw's' Railway Guides, 1841-1961 (issued annually)
Children of the Dead End Patrick MacGill, 1914
The Comic Bradshaw Angus Reach, 1848
The History of the Railway Connecting London and Birmingham Peter Lecount, 1839
The Life and Labours of Mr. Brassey Arthur Helps, 1872
The Life of George Stephenson Samuel Smiles, 1857
The Life of Joseph Locke Joseph Devey, 1862
The Midland Railway F.S. Williams, 1876
Our Iron Roads F.S. Williams, 1852 and other editions 1883 and 1888
Songs of a Navvy Patrick Macgill, 1912

Excellent modern works which are worth consulting are:

The Impact of Railways on Victorian Cities J.R. Kellet, Routledge and Kegan Paul, 1969
The Master Builders R.K. Middlemas, Hutchinson, 1963
The Railway Age Michael Robbins, Routledge and Kegan Paul, 1962
The Railway Navvies Terry Coleman, Hutchinson, 1965

ACKNOWLEDGMENTS

The author wishes to thank the following for their help in preparing this book:
David Mosley of the Education Department, The National Railway Museum, who made many useful suggestions on the structure of the book; Hilda Davies, who tracked down some obscure sources and Nick Harris and Ike Davies who provided additional photographs.

The author and publishers would like to thank the following for their kind permission to reproduce copyright illustrations: Barnaby's Picture Library, page 35; Brecon Museum, page 37; British Rail, page 30; Manchester Public Libraries, pages 8, 31; National Railway Museum, pages 11, 16, 20, 21, 23, 24, 24-25 (bottom), 44; Peter Newark's Historical Picture Service, pages 22-23 (bottom), 24-25 (top), 28-29 (bottom); NUR, pages 36-37, 38, 39; Michael Robbins, pages 26, 27 (from *The Railway Age* by Michael Robbins, published by Routledge & Kegan Paul); The Science Museum, London, pages 10, 14, 28, 29; Swindon Railway Museum, page 18, The Director, Wiltshire Library and Museum Service, page 19. The map on page 45 was drawn by Rudolph Britto.

The pictures on the front cover show: (top) first class and second class trains on the Liverpool and Manchester Railway, 1831 (Peter Newark's Historical Picture Service); (bottom left) a navvy on the tramp (The Science Museum, London); and (bottom right) part of an excursion notice, 1853 (from Michael Robbins, *The Railway Age*, published by Routledge & Kegan Paul).

Index

accidents
    to passengers 36-37
    to workers 11, 34-35
advertisements 26, 27, 28, 29, 30-31
ASRS: Amalgamated Society of Railway Servants *see under* Trade Unions
architecture 8, 20-21
ASLEF: Associated Society of Locomotive Engineers and Firemen *see under* Trade Unions

Brassey, Thomas 9, 10, 43
Brecon and Merthyr Railway 37
British Rail (BR) 3, 30, 44
Brunel, Isambard Kingdom 8, 43

Caledonian Railway 4, 10, 44
contractors 9, 10
    (*see also* Brassey, T.)

Dickens, Charles 15

Eastern Counties Railway 44
engineers 3, 7, 8-9, 10, 43 (*see also* Brunel, Locke, Stephenson G., Stephenson R., Trevithick)
excursions 3, 26-27

freight *see under* goods

goods 3, 4, 6, 18, 28-29
    coal 28
    fish 3, 29
    food 18
    milk 3
    raw materials 18
Grand Junction Railway 43, 44
Great Eastern Railway 20
Great Northern Railway 10, 27, 29, 34, 44
Great Western Railway (GWR) 3, 9, 19, 30, 31, 32, 33, 34, 37, 43, 44, 45

housing 14, 15, 19
Hudson, George 16, 17, 43

Lancashire and Yorkshire Railway 34, 44
Liverpool and Manchester Railway 22, 24, 28, 43, 44

Locke, Joseph 9, 43
locomotives
    diesel 4
    early 3, 7, 43
    electric 4
    Rocket 7, 43
    steam 3, 7
London and Birmingham Railway 10, 11, 15, 43, 44
London and Brighton Railway 44
London, Chatham and Dover Railway 26, 44
London and Greenwich Railway 3
London, Midland and Scottish Railway (LMS) 45
London and North Eastern Railway (LNER) 45
London and North Western Railway 20, 34, 44
London and Southampton Railway 44
London and Southwestern Railway 20, 44

MacGill, Patrick 11, 35, 42, 43
Manchester, Sheffield and Lincoln Railway 34, 44
Midland Railway 3, 20, 22, 23, 25, 34, 38, 43, 44
museums 5, 7

NUR: National Union of Railwaymen *see under* Trade Unions
navvies 10, 11, 42
    accidents to 11
    (*see also* railway workers)
North Eastern Railway 29, 33, 34, 44

Oxford Worcester and Wolverhampton Railway 27
Oystermouth Railway 6

Parliament 8, 12, 34, 40
    Acts of 3, 6, 9, 14, 22, 36, 45
passengers 4, 6, 18, 22-27
    accidents to 36-37
    advertising for 30-31
    coaches 6, 22, 23
    commuters 4, 18
    first class 22, 24, 25
    second class 22, 23
    third class 22, 23
Pen-y-Darren Tramroad 3, 7

RCA: Railway Clerks Association *see under* Trade Unions
railway companies 3, 8, 14, 16, 20, 32, 34 (*see also* under individual names, e.g. Great Western Railway)
railway lines
    building 8-11, 14, 15
    closures 4, 5, 42
    opposition to 12-13
railway mania 10, 16
railway stations 20-21
railway workers 4, 32-33
    accidents to 11, 34-35
    uniforms 32
    (*see also* navvies, Trade Unions)
Rocket see under locomotives
Ruskin, John 13

shares 16, 17
Sheffield 15, 21
Sheffield to Chesterfield Railway 14, 21, 28
sources 4-5
South Eastern Railway 44
Southern Railway (SR) 30, 45
Stephenson, George 7, 8, 43
Stephenson, Robert 9, 43
Stockton and Darlington Railway 3, 7, 43, 44
Surrey Iron Railway 28
Swindon 18-19, 33

Trade Unions 4, 38-41
    ASRS (later NUR): Amalgamated Society of Railway Servants 34, 38, 40, 41
    ASLEF: Associated Society of Locomotive Engineers and Firemen 38, 39
    RCA (later TSSA): Railway Clerks Association 38, 39, 41
tramroads 3, 6, 28 (*see also* Pen-y-Darren Tramroad, Oystermouth Railway, Surrey Iron Railway)
tramways *see under* tramroads
TSSA: Transport Salaried Staffs Association *see under* Trade Unions
Trevithick, Richard 3, 7, 43

Watt, James 3